Federal Air Marshals

BY KIRSTEN W. LARSON

amicus
high interest

Amicus High Interest is an imprint of Amicus
P.O. Box 1329, Mankato, MN 56002
www.amicuspublishing.us

Library of Congress Cataloging-in-Publication Data
Larson, Kirsten W.
Federal air marshals / by Kirsten W. Larson.
     pages cm. — (Protecting our people)
Audience: K to Grade 3.
Includes index.
ISBN 978-1-60753-984-1 (library binding) — ISBN 978-1-
68151-024-8 (ebook)
1. United States. Federal Air Marshal Service—Juvenile
literature. 2. Sky marshals—United States—Juvenile literature.
3. Airlines—Security measures—United States—Juvenile literature.
4. Law enforcement—Vocational guidance—United States—
Juvenile literature. I. Title.
HV8144.F37L37 2017
363.28'76—dc23

                                        2015033739

Editor: Wendy Dieker
Series Designer: Kathleen Petelinsek
Book Designer: Heather Dreisbach
Photo Researcher: Rebecca Bernin

Photo Credits: ColorBlind Images/Getty cover; Patti
McConville/Alamy 5; Barrie Harwood/Alamy 6; EdStock/
iStock 9; Juanmonino/iStock 10-11; age fotostock/Alamy 13;
Stuwdamdorp/Alamy 14; Rick Pisio/RWP Photography/Alamy
16-17; Kathryn Scott Osler/Getty 18; Associated Press 21; Tom
Mihalek 22-23; Associated Press 25; James Anderson/iStock
26; Air Force Tech. Sgt. Sean M.Worrell 29

Printed in the United States of America.

10 9 8 7 6 5 4 3 2 1

The author would like to thank former Federal Air Marshal Clay
Biles for his assistance with this book.

Table of Contents

Trouble in the Skies

Two hours into an airplane flight, a fight breaks out. When a woman leans back her seat, the man behind her gets angry. He does not have enough legroom. He argues and threatens. A flight attendant steps in. She tries to calm the man down. He yells even more. Then he follows her down the aisle. He grabs her. Uh-oh! Luckily two Federal Air Marshals are on the airplane.

A flight attendant helps passengers stay comfortable. Air marshals help when things get out of control.

Air marshals ask pilots to land the plane when there is an emergency.

 Did the man commit a crime?

Normally air marshals stay **undercover**. This time they need to act. The man is threatening the plane's crew. An air marshal's job is to protect them. The air marshals jump into action. They **restrain** the man. Meanwhile, the pilot lands the plane. The FBI arrests the man. He goes to jail.

 Yes. Threatening the flight crew is against the law. He could spend 20 years in jail.

A Day in the Life

Federal air marshals are like the sky police. Their job is to protect a plane's crew and passengers. But they are just one part of the Transportation Security Administration (TSA). The TSA works to keep danger off of planes, ferries, and trains. They make rules about what people can take on a plane. They inspect bags. They work hard, but if danger slips through, air marshals are ready to act.

TSA inspectors check for dangerous items in luggage before people get on the plane.

PLEASE
REMOVE LAPTOPS
AND PLACE IN
PLASTIC
CONTAINERS
THANK YOU

Air marshals fly undercover. They dress to blend in with other travelers. They act like travelers too. They watch a movie or read. They listen to music. Sometimes only the crew knows they are on board. It is a secret.

In the United States, air marshals fly in pairs. Flights to and from other countries have two pairs of air marshals.

Air marshals work to blend in. They are hard to spot.

Air marshals watch people on the plane. They look for clues that a person may cause trouble. Does anyone show signs of **stress**? When stressed, people may sweat. They might **fidget** too much or seem nervous.

Air marshals notice if a person looks out of place. Someone may wear a heavy coat in summer. Is he hiding something? Maybe. Air marshals watch these people closely.

These people all look like they belong on this plane. Air marshals spot people who look suspicious.

Workers at the airport help passengers book flights.

 What kind of gun do air marshals carry?

Air marshals restrain people who cause trouble or make threats. They carry guns, but they rarely use them. No air marshal has ever fired a gun in flight.

Air marshals travel a lot. If a trip is less than four hours, they fly home the same day. For **overseas** flights, they might rest a day.

 They carry 357s Sig Sauers.

There are fewer than 3,500 air marshals. They cannot be on every flight. Instead, they work only on the flights most at **risk**. Larger planes with more people have a greater risk. Air marshals also work on flights to and from some big cities. They also helped watch planes going to the Olympic Games in Greece.

An air marshal might be on a flight to a big city.

Flight staff and air marshals learn self-defense to keep safe in the air.

 Q Where do **recruits** start training?

Learning the Ropes

Anyone can train to become an air marshal. The TSA wants people from many backgrounds. Both men and women can be air marshals.

Training to become an air marshal takes four months. In the first part, recruits learn the basics of law enforcement. They work on fitness. Then they study the law. Finally they learn how to make arrests.

 They start in Artesia, New Mexico. Recruits train there for 35 days.

The next part of training takes place at a school in Atlantic City, New Jersey. Recruits learn to shoot. They practice **close combat**. They also learn how to take apart bombs.

This training center has an old plane to use on the ground. Inside, recruits practice keeping flights safe. People pretend to take over the airplane. Air marshals practice fighting back.

 Where did the practice plane come from?

Air marshals practice shooting guns at the range in Atlantic City.

 Delta Airlines gave it to the air marshals.

Learning to shoot is very important. Many people are on an airplane. If air marshals must shoot, they cannot make a mistake. They learn to shoot from 75 feet (23 m) away. They even practice shooting from behind seats. Bang! Bang! Air marshals are some of the best shooters.

Fake plane seats help air marshals practice shooting safely.

Working with Others

Air marshals have jobs on the ground too. Some air marshals work at airports. They might help keep traveling world leaders safe. They work security in emergencies too. During Hurricane Katrina in 2005, planes could not leave New Orleans. People were stranded at the airport. Air marshals helped keep things orderly.

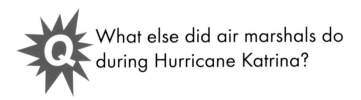

Q What else did air marshals do during Hurricane Katrina?

The Russian prime minister gets on a helicopter in Virginia. Air marshals might help keep him safe.

 They made sure no one had weapons in the airport. They also made sure only airport workers were in the control tower.

Air marshals might help keep
people safe at ferry stations.
They are trained to protect.

The TSA keeps people safe on trains, ferries, and subways, too. Sometimes air marshals work in those places. They help screen passengers. They use bomb-sniffing dogs to check for explosives. They use machines to scan for bombs. They work to stop **terrorists**.

Sometimes teams of air marshals work with police at music concerts, rodeos, and other big events. They keep crowds safe.

Protecting Our People

Federal air marshals keep us safe. They watch over us when we travel. They blend into the crowd, so you might not see them. But when they need to, they act.

Air marshals fly the skies every day. They fly even more than pilots and other crew to keep us safe. Are they heroes? Yes!

Air marshals arrive to help keep the people at the airport safe during a hurricane.

Glossary

close combat To fight with someone nearby; fighters may or may not use weapons in close combat.

fidget To keep moving and wiggling out of boredom or nervousness.

overseas A country that is across an ocean from you.

recruit A person who is taking tests and trying to get into a job or program.

restrain To hold someone down and stop them from doing something.

risk The possibility of harm or danger.

stress Nervousness, strain, or pressure.

terrorist A person using violence or threats to frighten people.

undercover Working in secret.

Read More

Schaefer, Lola M. *Airplanes in Action.* Transportation Zone. Mankato, Minn.: Capstone Press, 2012.

Woods, Michael and Mary B. Woods. *Air Disasters.* Disasters Up Close. Minneapolis, Minn.: Lerner Publishing Group, 2007.

Woog, Adam. *Careers in Homeland Security.* Law and Order Jobs. New York: Cavendish Square Publishing, 2014.

Websites

Federal Law Enforcement | What is an Air Marshal
http://www.federallawenforcement.org/air-marshal/what-is-an-air-marshal/

Inside Look: Federal Air Marshal Service
https://youtu.be/rv6O__vRTaM

Index

About the Author

Kirsten W. Larson has written dozens of books
and articles for young people. She loves to travel
and would like to thank the Federal Air Marshals
for keeping her safe. Visit her website at
www.kirsten-w-larson.com.